Praise for *Faraway Hometown*

In this collection, Zhihua Wang crafts delicate poems that examine the speaker's inner life with courage and humility. With a focus on everyday details, the poems provide an intimate portrait as the speaker wrestles with a question common to many of us today— "how far am I from home?" In the quest to establish roots both literal and figurative, the poet offers up hard-won wisdom nestled in well-penned words.
—Sandy Longhorn, author of *The Alchemy of My Mortal Form*

These poems are a gift. *Faraway Hometown* signals the arrival of an utterly original voice in poetry, one that will be captivating us for a long time.
—Stephanie Vanderslice, author of *The Lost Son*

Zhihua Wang's beautiful first collection asks us to consider the urgent and the quotidian often at once—in the cycles of nature, technology, medicine and the maternal. The precision and candor of Wang's voice provides warm humanity and always surprising insights. *Faraway Hometown* also offers constant reminders of how essential poetry is in negotiating our landscapes.
—Kevin Henderson, Professor of English and Chair of Languages and Literature, Drury University

Faraway Hometown

Poems

Zhihua Wang

Three Pines Press
St Petersburg, FL 33713
www.threepinespress.com
threepinespress@gmail.com

EU Representation
R. Vencu
Negoi 58b, Sibiu, RO-550275
richard.vencu@gmail.com

9 8 7 6 5 4 3 2 1

Printed in the United States of America

□ This edition is printed on acid-free paper that meets the American National Standard Institute Z39.48 Standard.
Distributed in the United States by Three Pines Press.

Cover design: Photograph by Gryffin M. Arrangement by Brent Christopher Wulf.

Library of Congress Cataloging-in-Publication Data

Names: Wang, Zhihua, 1973- author
Title: Faraway hometown : poems / Zhihua Wang.
Description: St Petersburg, FL : Three Pines Press, [2026]
Identifiers: LCCN 2025043438 | ISBN 9781931483872 paperback
Subjects: LCGFT: Autobiographical poetry
Classification: LCC PS3623.A465 F37 2026 | DDC 811/.6--dc23/eng/20251202
LC record available at https://lccn.loc.gov/2025043438

Contents

Deciphering Mysteries

Faraway Hometown

Seeking Happiness

Preface

A well-known television host
once said,
"I've given my best
to my audience."

A famous film director
once said,
"My best was given
to my actors."

I'm nobody,
but like a bee busy
with its honey,
a flower waiting
for its fruit,

I put my best here.

Deciphering Mysteries

Blinds

If I could be you,
drifting at ease
between days and nights,
between light and darkness.

Could watch the bright
new world
with eyes wide open.

Could shut down everything,
back to the interior,
to peace,
in just a turn, a blink.

Cherries

How do you manage this?
Skin rich in red,
pulp more sensual
and intense
after a bite.
Dark juice runs
on my fingers,
lingers on my lips,
as thick as red wine,
but with a flavor
mostly mild.

My Tomato Vines

I indulge myself in looking
at your every leaf, every bud,
and every branch. You'll never
refuse my gaze, never be shy,
impatient, or run away
like my child.

I'm shocked how tall
you shot up for a night. I ponder
how much water you need for a day.
I count how many flowers
are in bloom, and how many
bear signs of fruit.

I make compost
and hope my rice-rinse water
will nourish you. I remove suckers,
trim leaves, and build tripods
for you to extend
with grace.

Sometimes you show no change,
but still full of vigor, I figure
you're deepening your roots.
Yellow blossoms keep emerging,
I must admit that not all
turn to a tomato.

You teach me that to bloom,
I need to keep climbing,
to fruit, I need a strong stalk.
When the little dome
is on the way, the flower
shrinks into a prelude.

Every day, I expect you as much
as you expect me. My eyes
caress you, my heart
talks to you. When the wind
passes, I see you answering me
in laughter and nods.

Photo by Paul La Rosa on Unsplash

Studying in the Library

A boiled egg,
a banana,
and a steamed bun

tucked in my backpack,
weigh as much
as my books and laptop.

After reading a chapter,
finishing a critique,
or drafting a paper,

I'll feed myself one,
like a master
training a dog.

Digging in My Poems in the Morning

Urged by the need to please my heart
and placate my blood, I open old lines
and jot down new sprouts—like Narcissus
viewing himself in the mirror, like

a hearty breakfast waiting at my table:
honey, bread, milk—a feast after a fast,
nectar aged by time and yeast.
Ideas weighed, voices chewed, words

combed smooth with sheen. Hands knock
them into keepsakes of black and white,
like fresh produce on display, like what
I care for is tended, like applying

lotion to my face, my neck—I've touched
every nook and cranny, inside and out.

Insomnia

This morning,
I find myself waking
calmly in bed—
God has finally pulled
me in, for several hours
of sleep, in His haven.

After fighting with insomnia,
I finally won.
dancing aerobics
for thirty minutes
at 2 a.m.

With all the heat,
sweat, and endorphins
it generated, I slipped
into my warm quilt.

Eyes closed,
the melody still echoing
in my mind,
the bed became a boat,
swaying—
soon, I was in.

Jogging

Whether I run like antelope or pig,
it doesn't matter, so long as my knees
can bend, my soles can lift, I can
bob and hit the ground without pause

for a set period. The first half
of the journey is to test my patience,
I keep up like boiling water
in a tea kettle, till all the particles

begin to stir, till the heart beats faster,
the breath shorter, till sweat forms,
then trickles down, like steam
rising, I blow my whistle—

I'm rejuvenated, inflated, like the cloud
on top of the world, floating.

Wait

Arrive early to check in,
wait for the nurse
to call your name,
wait for the doctor
to enter the room.

Bring a book,
but never bother to open it.
The mind strains, as if an alarm
is about to ring, a sentence
to be announced.

Wait to take the test,
wait for the result,
then another…like a bus
arriving at a station,
drops some off,
picks up the new.

Footsteps far and near,
doors open and shut,
meeting and parting words
at your eardrum,
knocks at a door,
but not yours.

Wait is a way
to defeat will, till an hour
is not an hour, and you
are not you. Like life—

a mala strung
with waiting, at times,
no bead is held,
only the bare thread.

To My Surgeon

Two orderlies push my gurney in,
parallel with the table. I scoop
myself over, limbs buckled,

a heavy pad strapped to my abdomen.
I see masked faces—eyes
not yours, my heart pounds.

Soon I black out.
The rest I can only imagine—
under halogen lamps, they shave

my armpit, you mark the places
to be cut. Wherever the scalpel's edge
trails, blood runs in red rivulets.

Gloved hands excise flesh
gone wrong, fingers interweaving
with forceps and needle holder

to suture the cuts. I often go over this,
wondering how I abused my body
to make you carve on me.

I wonder if you care about
your work—the lines you draw,
the wounds you sew—

they're performing
and healing well.
I touch them every day.

The Nature Inside Me

Veins and organs in me
are rivers and mountains on earth.
Scientists decipher mysteries
that I never see through.

Bacteria battle,
cells die and renew,
every nerve has a will,
every cycle is law and order.

As sun I rise,
as moon I fall,
the epitome of nature resides,
limited resource, limited time.

In nature, I seek remedy,
never resorted to the version
inside me, never loved it
enough, never saw it with awe.

Side Effects

People are talking about which vaccine
to take: Pfizer, Moderna, or Johnson.
They search online and compare words
for the one with the least side effects.

I delay again and again for my test,
afraid of the chemicals, the radiation.
The best choice is to have no choice,
take what there is. Tell me one thing

that is pure good—food wears out organs,
sleep steals my time, exercise hurts
my bones, reading blurs my vision.
And love—it breaks my heart. As for

this poem, it amplifies moments, examines
nature, and makes me more judgmental.

My Healing

My healing, circuitous,
like a fly—
how many loops
must it make
to land
on that crumb?

Peach

Have you ever eaten
a peach
with a split pit?

Her heart
is broken, yet she
still looks rosy
and tastes sweet.

Photo by Katherine Hood on Unsplash

Modern Technology Illusions

1

I try to use Ctrl + F
to search for a word in my paper book.

I try to rewind
what you just said.

2

In a group chat,
voices don't infringe
my personal space,
they infringe my cyberspace.

3

A room without internet,
a swimming pool with no water.

4

If you don't answer
my email the first time,
I give up—soon,
it will be buried in your inbox.

5

A one-word email
weighs the same
as any other.

6

My mouse clicks,
my time slips.

7

Calls, emails, messages—
none of them
reaches me faster
if I turn off my phone.

8

Tell me how to turn off
a touchless tap
that drips water.

9

Need a blackout evening,
so I can feel the real darkness.

10

When I sit at my desk,
glued to my screen,
glimpsing a dog
and its walker outside,
I feel they are free.

11

When I get out of my car,
I feel free.

Wet Floor

I often bump
into a wet floor sign
where the floor is not wet.

I figure it's mandatory
to remind people
of slip and fall,

but not a breach
of rule if it stays put
when dry.

So it stands stately
in the middle
of the ground,

in plain sight,
telling a lie.

2020

1

It's October now,
I am still listening to the song
"Beautiful Springtime."
It seems the spring
of 2020 never came.

2

The moon must love
my daughter's window
more as it often has songs
flying out of it.

3

I'm in love with my bed now.
Every time I lie on my pillow,
wrapped in my comforter,
I think of him.

4

Poems are flowers
I pass along my road.
I gather them into words
and send them away—
when they're opened,
I hope—the fragrance
is still there.

5

I used to believe
most of the world
thought like me.
Now I know it's only
half. But I should still cheer
even if the win is by a hair.

The Last Day of Summer

Like clothes taken off
layer by layer before shower,
now it has reached the end—
what is left for me?

No matter how bountiful
the days were at the beginning,
they all slip, like water
through my fingers.

I planted some ideas,
they haven't bloomed yet.
Some grass prospers well,
and growing wild.

Tomorrow is said
to be wind and rain,
tonight is a river
I don't want to wade.

Cat Orange

1

You were almost three
when we adopted you,
pampered by a loving lady
at the beginning of your life,
now trapped in three pairs
of green hands.

2

You literally sniff everything
and I feel nothing.
Only when you smell the flowers,
I feel different.

3

I'm immersed in learning
my second language,
you challenge me by talking
with the only word
in your vocabulary.

4

In the morning, when
my daughter is still asleep,
I hear you croon
at her window.

Your soft, turning,
and tactful voice is different
from the demanding meows
you give us parents.

She treats you with her songs
and notes from her keyboard,
so you speak to her
in a different tone—

it's your understanding
of music. They are
your songs.

5

With me, you scream
in order to play outside.
You sing
while trotting back.

You dash into my room
before I close the door.
You crouch outside,
beg for your bedtime snack.

Sometimes, I see you in me,
sometimes, I see me in you.

6

Not sure of our own tomorrow,
I put your cutest pictures
in a group chat,
hoping someone is willing
to rehome you.

After two months,
the guy who once queried,
confirms that he wants you,
I know our real separation

is around the corner,
my tears run
unbridled.

7

In what way
will you know
or should we do
to let you know
that we are seeing you
off today—

like marrying off a kid
and never seeing him come back.

Your new home master
will drive hours to pick you up—

there're many cues in the air,
many talks among us, and many
are addressed to you—

but you will never know

until the moment comes—

until we place you in your carrier
          zip it up, and lift you
into a new car,

until you think back
on today
later.

8

We have you
          in our pictures
and videos,

you have us
          in your memory.

Photo by Juan Manuel Sanchez on Unsplash

Faraway Hometown

My Black Hair

I'll grow my black hair long,
let it be wavy naturally
and hang freely.
I love its romantic feeling,
also for my not pretty
and a little melancholy face.

My black hair
is a wreath in the dreams
of girls, letting me
flutter in the wind
or swirl in dance
to draw you
into my flying whirlpool.

Till one day,
I confirm that you've stayed
and will never move apart,
I'll consider cutting it,
also cutting off
my numerous
youthful thoughts.

Jujubes

When I have a yard,
I won't grow grass
just to mow it for the noise.

Nor will I raise chickens
for eggs—there are plenty
in the markets.

When I have a yard,
I'll plant jujube trees—cultivate
them around my house.

They're fond of sunshine
and heat, but not afraid of cold,
nor drought.

Little yellow flowers
bloom in summer, clusters
of jujubes dangle in autumn.

Fruit the size of an "OK"
gesture, turns from green
to brown when ripe.

Skin smooth with luster,
pulp firm, juicy,
tastes like maple syrup.

Even though very mellow
they never fall and rot,
but dry themselves

into soft, wrinkled dates,
luring people to pick
and preserve.

Choice

Unconsciously,
I've chosen a difficult road—
going forward, thorns.
going back, I don't see my home.

By now, I can only wish
that I can be firm
and move on.

Don't ask about me.
Assume I've many things
in this world forgotten,
like festivals, travels,
and the enthusiasm
of a reunion.

People are adorning
their lives, to cheer others
or please themselves.
I only want to be left alone,
with one heart
sinking
to the bottom.

Sobs of the Train

On a rainy winter night, a train passes the small town I live. Its whistle echoes like a forlorn sob, carrying my thoughts away. Everywhere, trains sing the same sad song. They remind me that there are people on the road tonight.

They remind me that I, too, am on a journey—how far am I from home? How many miles have I traveled to get here? Once I leaped onto a moving train, I couldn't stop, I couldn't turn back.

Before the journey, everything I envisioned was like bubbles in a dream. After I set out, everywhere I went overgrown with brambles. I return to every smile, pay attention to every sound, ruminate on every encounter, yet still see a world I cannot understand.

Why did I throw away a familiar world? Wasn't I seeking a better life? The differences I longed for; the differences I don't belong to. If life is viewed as a whole, are there really any differences?

Tonight, I have a harbor I call home, away from sleepless nights, the dark outside, the cold, windy, muddy road. I can snuggle into my cozy bed beneath the warm orange light. Yet who knows tomorrow, where the train will go, and where my heart will follow?

Take a Bow

When you're still glittering
on stage for the final curtain call,
I've retracted from my seat
and left the hall.

Forgive me for leaving you
without a word—if later,
you'll search for me in the crowd
and hope to meet my eyes.

Afraid of weaving through
people, also don't know
how to face you
after the makeup and costume.

Take a bow—to you,
in my heart. The road ahead
is dim, but you're a full moon,
shining in my world.

Mother

I call you forever
in my most painful moments,
but I won't tell you.

My eyes are always wet,
thinking of my inconsiderate past,
but I won't let you know.

You're the coordinates of my life,
marking my starting point
and tracing my every move.

You're my farthest
hometown—the closest place
my heart dwells upon.

The umbilical cord we shared
was never cut—
each time we part,
it ties us together.

Flying

Flying—
perhaps it's for that one day,
I'll stay by your side,
knowing
I no longer need to fly.

Steamed Bread

I inherit it, and inject my ideal of making splendid bread:
water, flour, yeast, cage-free eggs, no-sugar-added bread.

Mix them all, I can't wait for the dough to rise. Crush it—
it grows again. Do I expect more than my unadorned bread?

Knead it by hand, divide it, roll it, shape it like a flower
or stuff it with bean paste, set aside to prove rounded bread.

Place them in the steamer. Vapor expands each inner beehive
to full size. Time and temperature decide puffed bread.

Gaze at them, feel their warm, moist, and dappled skin,
break one, bring it to mouth. Oh, elastic, chewy, revered bread.

Like being a chef, Zhihua? Yes! This process is more than healing.
If you ask who lasts—I, or the steamed bread? Steamed bread.

Photo by Hewq on Pixabay

Ode to Eyes

Eyes are the instruments
I play with you—like a bow,
gliding on the strings
of the cello.

Like a ball, running
on the field, kicked
and bounced back
before it shoots the goal.

Like ponds of water,
carrying waves underneath,
they bulge, dilate,
and discharge electricity.

Gaze straight or winding,
they long to clash and go
astray. Flitting or firm,
they know where to locate

and when to tangle.
Everything else is covered—
eyes are the only nudity
we exchange.

There is a PIN Number

There is a PIN number
in your mood, it changes
every time we meet.

A Walker

I walk into a road
under construction.
A large sign ahead says,
"Road closed."

I feel I can still pass.
Maybe it doesn't mean
for people—it means
for vehicles?

Here is America—
a country on wheels.
Trails are for people,
roads are for cars.

When they say
it's several minutes away,
they mean by car.
I tell myself to stay calm

when I step into a street
with whooshing traffic,
but no sidewalks
for a pedestrian.

Run

Sometimes I run,
not because I love it,
but because I'm not
satisfied with my speed.
I'm still so ignorant
in this new world.
I'm still falling
behind my plan.
So I push myself
to run, knowing
the endorphins released
from the workout
will slow me down.

Why I Cry

I know why I cry—
because I've glimpsed
the shadow of death.
It hides somewhere in the corner,
waiting for the moment
to seize me.
If I fall suddenly,
who will come for me?

I know why I cry—
because it's time
to say goodbye.
Days are passing,
mysteries are unraveling,
the light we struck in our sky
is extinguishing—
I'm dying in your eyes.

If I See You Again

I'll tell you two things:
first, I'm leaving.
I'll look closely at your eyes
for your reaction.

Whether you look like nothing,
or lower your head in sorrow,
I'll tell you the other:
I love you.

The former, a road
I blaze toward another sky,
the latter, a bird, pent up
in my ribcage for long—

I would see it free
when I leave.

My Old Potted Money Tree

I hope you can feel me
standing beneath
your high-rise balcony,
in dust and tears.

We were once a family,
lived together for a decade.
One day I said goodbye
to you for good, to wander.

Years later, I feel lucky
to come back alive,
looking up at you
through the dim moonlight.

Your greenness,
is just what I wanted.
When we're separated
by an ocean, each faces

an unpredictable fate,
the deepest hope
is no more than we both
in this world, breathe.

September

There aren't many days
left in September—the month
of my birth, like a home
I visit once a year.

When summer fled
with its heat, cooled breezes
used to whisper at my ears,
I'm from afar, want to roam?

I followed and arrived
at a place farther than
my dream, with a calendar
fuller than I can cope with.

Need a time slot—go to
the meadow, sit in the middle,
watch the insects hustle,
feel the sunshine

milder, the sky higher,
and give wind a chance—
when it waves the grass,
it strokes me, too.

Reunion

If I row a boat, sailing
along the river every day,
will there be a day
I can swing into your dream?

If I bow my head, climbing
over a mountain a day,
will there be a day
I can stand before you,
face to face?

Are you also looking out
from the hilltop,
the trail of my arrival?

Are you also, for this
reunion, counting over
days, nights, and stars?

Old Classmates

I hesitate to admit it—
my heart still feels young,
though time knows
we've lived over forty years.
Thirty years of trials
may have shaped me
into someone new.
Moving forward,
our faces gather more wrinkles.

Why does reunion
make my heart race?
Why is our time together
so fleeting, so warm?
Because our youthful ignorance
is preserved in memory—
we are the ones
who witnessed
each other's tender youth.

An MFA Student from China

1

"So, you're from China,
and write poetry—in English?"
Often, people ask.

"Yes," I reply.
"I make them short,
so fewer mistakes."

Sometimes I think:
If poetry is broken English,
that's what I'm good at.

2

The good thing
about being in a pandemic
is if I don't understand others,
I can blame the mask.

3

After my reading performance
in class, a peer came to tell me
that he liked my accent.
The problem was—
I didn't know that I had an accent.

4

Before teaching my class,
I felt the need to go to the restroom
multiple times.

Emails from my students
rushed in, telling me
why they were unable to come.

I think I need to be more patient—
sometimes, it's for them to learn,
sometimes, it's for me.

5

I've heard people say
that when you speak English
in your dream, your mindset
has shifted to the English mode.

A pen and a blank notebook
are tucked constantly beside my pillow
to catch the lines that might
emerge in my dreams.

Words overlap or stay far apart
while I scribble in the middle
of my sleep, but see—
sometimes, they're in English:

Words are eyes in the blinds.

Head on the pillow seeks
the same level as the bed.

Someday I will see it,
like seers see the seas.

Seeking Happiness

Trees

Salute every tree
that I pass by.

I move constantly,
you're there all the time.

Your abundance
often slows my steps.
Must I set forth endlessly
in order to flourish?

Maybe your pursuit
is the sky, so you reach up
to your best, as I
imagine happiness

is always ahead
on my road.

Photo by Johann Siemens on Unsplash

Trees at My Window

Every migration
is like a permanent separation.
The maples that change
the color of my window
have imprinted themselves
in my mind
as an everlasting picture.

Wherever I go,
trees are my life's companions
I will always look to—
birds singing,
leaves falling,
even though everything is lost,
everything comes back.

Dream

My dream is to have a house
of my own, with forest trails
in its surroundings. Every day,
I will look forward to a walk outside.

My dream is to have a large table,
on it are all the books I love,
and my job is to write my poems.

I dream the sky is blue,
the sun is warm, water is sweet,
food is green, the internet is close,
the world is at a distance,
the only thing I feel short of is time.

Time

I

You see my white hair,
I see your wrinkles.
After a couple of decades,
when we meet by chance
on the street, we lament
the ruthlessness of time.

Yet we're young
in our own minds,
because every morning
we meet ourselves
in our mirrors, and never
see that big a difference.

II

You were once my best friend,
walked with me hand in hand,
talking about seeing
the outside world together.

Little by little,
I grew slower,
you never changed your steps.

I looked back
now and then,
you never turned your head.

Trying to keep you
at my side, you strode forward
and left me behind.

Watching your hurried back,
I saw you'd again
been joined
by many new friends.

III

You're always on my mind,
but I've never owned you—

like the longest hand
on a clock,
I don't own the past,
I don't own the future.
Ever in the present,
I'm just a walker.

On the Window

On the window
of Brickley's Ice Cream shop,
they write:
Closed for the season—
see you next year.

Time has never
been so sweet to wait.

Goal on the Trail

With an "Excuse me,"
you pass me, allowing me
a glimpse of your profile
to guess your age,
and a full view of your back
to appreciate your beauty.

You're about sixty,
in a blue shirt and black shorts.
Your long, straight legs
and slim waist
move as light as a bird.
Not a spot of fat.

Suddenly, I have a goal.
I decide to follow you—
keep the same rhythm as you
and outpace others too.
On the loop of the trail,
your figure, my flagship.

After one lap, I'm out of breath;
you still glide as before.
Not everyone can be a miracle,
I sigh, and let you go.

Back to strolling,
I greet the clouds and pause
for the flowers, nothing feels
wrong until another "Excuse me"
makes me freeze—
you pass by me, again.

Daughter

For the many days we've shared,
I'm able to hear you sing—
humming songs by my side
as if confiding to me in melody.

I'm able to watch you draw—
colorful hearts and balloons
captioned with "I love you, Mom"
and tucked into my closed laptop.

And I'm able to see you play—
while I'm lost in my work,
you hide beneath my bed, eating
the M&M that fell there earlier.

Yes, I'm able to see you grow—
from loud cries to shy smiles,
from a little one to be carried
to being yourself in every aspect.

You're an angel falling into
my world, being my bliss, my pride,
my idol, my friend, sharing
with me a life with no regret.

Playing Badminton with My Daughter

Hearts fly with the birdie,
eyes trace its trajectory,
legs run or leap,
bats extend
like a magnet absorbing iron.

We make a thread
between us
weaving in the air,

like a skein of wool
rolling into a ball—

with angle and stretch,
we keep our yarn
spinning.

Pen

I keep you handy
in case I feel unsure
of remembering things
or want to scribble down ideas
rushed in suddenly.

You lie in the harbor
of my thumb and forefinger—
I long to hold you there,
a sign I have words to trail
or stories to tell.

Compared to the cursor
flickering on the screen,
fingertips dancing on keyboard,
you're just small. Yet you
focus my strength

when I write,
feel my heart throb
when I draw, record the mess
of my thoughts, and stand by
my truthfulness.

Poetry

Language of the weak—
flowers growing
on cliffs, in the Gobi,
or between cracks
of rocks,

watered
by a humble heart.

Photo by Mariagrazia Viezzer on Unsplash

Submitting Work

When I receive a rejection,
I send out new submissions—
my way of striking back.

I worry about declines,
but I fear more
running out of ammunition.

Appreciating Poetry

To love a poet
is an easy thing,
so long as they have one poem
that truly touches me.

To love a poem
is an easy thing,
so long as it has one line
that truly changes me.

I don't own jewels,
those poems
are the precious stones
that I carry often.

I haven't seen meteors,
those lines
are falling stars,
flashing across my sky.

Life

I

Maybe you'll surprise me
for a brief moment,
but I've waited
for a whole night.

Maybe you've arranged
for me a common growth,
but I've watched for it
in my entire blooming season.

Maybe you'll give me
an earthly love,
a mundane world,
and a future that we all foresee—

but I'll give you everything,
and devote myself
to you, always,
in full.

II

When the sun is shining bright,
will it connect you to the past?
The song floats on the small playground
on campus, under the basketball
hoops, our flying dreams.

We carry our dreams
and stumble forward.
Sooner or later, there will be bumps
ahead that make us fall,
sometimes because of ourselves,
sometimes, someone else.

Life, always at a certain point,
in a certain way, lets us hurt.

My Sleep

Since I've gotten used to sleeping
on the floor, I figure I can travel
around the world now. The nights

tossing in strange beds and beddings
won't be a scene. Everywhere
will be the same: hard and flat.

I only need my small pillow,
my thin pad, and my warm comforter
along the journey. Every time

I roll them up into a bundle,
and squeeze them into my suitcase,
I feel I've packed with me, my sleep.

I'll Celebrate

I'll celebrate
the good news today,
since tomorrow
I'll take it for granted.

Ode to My Blender

If there's a color for the day, it starts
with you. The green smoothie isn't always
green. It can be pink, yellow, ivory,
or more. Today is reddish-purple
out of the blue, equalized by water
and a heap of chopped fruits and vegetables.

Kiwis sour, carrots hard, celery grassy,
grapes sugary—to please a fickle human's
palate is no simple art. But when
they're whirled in your boisterous
vortex, settle into a shade, and poured
into my glass tumbler, it's a delicious

concoction with every essence I crave.
God created a world, you blend one new.

So Much Just Happened

So much just happened
in a new poem, yet the world
remains the same.

My Reflection

There's a person I haven't
seen today, a person who's engaged
with herself in the kitchen this morning,

a person who was nurtured
by a full night's sleep, every inch
of her skin must be glossy. A glimpse

of her glory in the bathroom
mirror doesn't suffice. I long to meet
her in my portable, circular, dual-sided,

3x magnifying looking glass. Hoist
the blinds, lift the window, in nature's
light, I sit before her, examine her,

stroke her—even with the added lines,
the trials and errors, she still holds
my full attention, holds my hope

for miracles, knowing I'll search
for her best form to the end, and she
will love me, every day, a little bit more.

No More One at a Time

When my mouth
is chewing,
my eyes are also searching
for something
to feed.

I end up
gluing my eyes
to the screen of my laptop
every time
I'm having a meal.

In the Ends We Pursue

Maybe we need to be far wealthier,
so even a small portion
of our giving means a lot.

Maybe we need to be far more famous,
so we can lift someone
worthy of true notice.

Maybe we need to be far deeper
in thought, so we can teach
a line others will remember.

Maybe we need to be far kinder,
so even our smallest act
can warm a stranger's heart.

Why Old Friends Go

I know why
my old friends go,
because new ones
are coming,
because I can't hold
too much love—
like a bottle of water,
when it's full,
it will spill.

Last Night

Last night,
countless lines of poetry
emerged in my dream.

This morning,
I found it was
a window in my room
left open.

Best Life

Eat less for supper,
and rest early
when my brain
can't absorb.

Lying in bed,
dreaming of the food
I love to cook
and the words
I long to pore over.

The next day
when I get up,
I'll always be reminded
of that hunger.

Tucker Creek Trail

I reach out to you to dab some sunshine
on my skin, to plant some landscapes

in my vision. The stream is rarely
full, only on rainy days, yet the woods

block swathes of secular residence,
and make my excursion like a dream.

My steps rhyme with my heartbeats,
my song lingers on my lips:

change a space, I'll see places
with no rejections…

now all I need is to pick a direction—
the west leads to a clearing

I've not dabbled in. The south hosts
a tree shimmering with persimmons.

Moving forward, I can swing
by Walmart for my anti-aging black grapes.

Remember to calculate the to
and back time, they should be equal.

Remember the less I carry,
the brisker my journey.

The earth is a rough sphere,
and this life, a tough circle,

yet the moment I set foot
on you, road sprawls ahead

smooth and even, as beautiful
as I ever wanted it to be.

Epilogue

When I was young,
I dreamed of roaming
to faraway, new places.

My dream came true.
Later, I see what I gain—
a hometown faraway.

Photo by Hans Veth on Unsplash

About this Work

Faraway Hometown is a collection of poems about a Chinese woman's life in the United States. The speaker, whom I often see as myself, came here to study, fulfilling a long-held dream of seeing the outside world. Yet she never anticipated the challenges of living in an entirely different place. Therefore, pursuing dreams and seeking comfort are two threads unconsciously woven into the poems.

The title *Faraway Hometown* came to me as I sat on a bench outside an auto repair shop in Conway, Arkansas, during the COVID-19 pandemic. I watched the flat, open landscape stretch to meet the sky across a four-lane street, and it reminded me of Wuhan, my hometown in China. Though I worried about the people there and longed to visit, it was nearly impossible for me to return at that time. From another perspective, I had arrived at a place where I could pursue my passion for language and writing. In this sense, I also see the United States as a new hometown.

The collection begins with the poem "Preface," which describes my general understanding of poetry. To me, poetry is a form of meditation—a spiritual practice. It embodies my best moments—beautiful moments, insightful moments, or moments of discovery. I try to use words to revive these moments and keep them as alive as possible, hoping that one day I can share them with others.

The book is divided into three sections to create pauses in the reading experience. The first section, *Decipher Mysteries*, centers on the speaker's present, navigating a new world, embracing its freshness and challenges, and striving for balance. The second, *Faraway Hometown*, explores her roots and heritage—the people and places she longs for, as well as the contrast she feels between two different worlds. The final section, *Seeking Happiness*, highlights the elements she wishes to carry forward: self-care, self-control, and self-reflection, all in pursuit of a fulfilling life.

As the closing poem, "Tucker Creek Trail" reflects the speaker's inner journey. She has reached a deeper understanding of life, finding beauty and fulfillment in the path she has chosen, it is a happy ending.

Finally, I included a short poem as an epilogue, one that came to me while I was sitting in front of the auto repair shop. It echoes the collection's title and mirrors the speaker's realization: the farther I go, the farther my hometown becomes.

Acknowledgments

I am deeply grateful to Professor Sandy Longhorn, who generously taught me poetry and helped me greatly improve the work in this collection. I would also like to thank all my professors at the University of Central Arkansas—Stephanie Vanderslice, John Vanderslice, Mark Spitzer, Jennie Case, M Shelly Conner, Bob May, and Cristine Busser. Your influence is embedded within this collection.

Heartfelt thanks go to all my professors at Drury University: Kevin Henderson, Jo Van Arkel, Peter Meidlinger, Charlyn Ingwerson, Katherine Gilbert, Patrick Moser, Greg Booker… and my supervisor at the library, Barbi Dickensheet. Each of you inspired me to pursue this path.

I also thank all my professors at the University of Rhode Island for the opportunity to continue my writing studies. I am especially indebted to Carolyn Betensky, Peter Covino, and Talvikki Ansel for their guidance and encouragement in my work.

In addition, I extend my gratitude to all my teachers, classmates, and friends, both in the U.S. and China, for their immense support. Just to mention a few: Lorraine Gardner, Kumiko Nagai, Mirene Oliveira, Wang Jingfang 王静芳, Guo Jing 郭靖, Hu Liping 胡丽萍, and Li Shiping 李士平. And to my family—thank you for standing by me with patience through every step of this journey.

Last but not least, I would like to express my sincere gratitude to Three Pine Press and her executive editor, Livia Kohn, for believing in this manuscript and providing it with a wonderful home.

And to you, my reader—thank you. I hope you enjoy this book.

Previously Published

Academy of the Heart and Mind: "Wait," "Side Effect," "Take a Bow," "Mother," "Dream," "Trees," "Trees at My Window"

Across the Margin: "Pen," "My Reflection," "Life"

Aji Magazine: "Wet Floor," "To My Surgeon," "The Nature Inside Me"

Autumn Sky Poetry Daily: "Steamed Bread"

Cold Moon Journal: "So Much Just Happened"

The Curator: "My Sleep"

Currents: "Insomnia"

Down in the Dirt: "Appreciating Poetry"

The Drabble: "Choice"

Eunoia Review: "Tucker Creek Trail," "Modern Technology Illusions"

The Indianapolis Review: "Jogging"

King River Press: "I'll Celebrate"

Last Leaves Magazine: "Studying in the Library," "Digging in My Poems in the Morning," "My Tomato Vines," "Jujube," "My Old Potted Money Tree"

Midwest Zen: "Time"

Moss Piglet Zine: "Ode to My Blender"

North of Oxford: "Ode to Eyes"

Nurture: "Playing Badminton with My Daughter"

The Literary Hatchet: "September," "If I See You Again"

The Penwood Review: "Peach"

The Piker Press: "Best Life," "Submitting Work," "Why Old Friends Go"

Poetry Super Highway: "Blinds," "Cherries," "Poetry"

Pure Slush: "Cat Orange"

San Pedro River Review: "The Last Day of Summer"

Salamander Magazine: "An MFA Student from China"

Scarlet Dragonfly Journal: "There Is a PIN Number"

Tipton Poetry Journal: "Run"

WestWard Quarterly: "Goal on the Trail"

Writers Resist: "2020"

Previously Published